DATE DUE	

Reading Essentials
in Social Studies

SYMBOLS OF A NATION

Washington, D.C.

Thomas S. Owens

Perfection Learning®

Editorial Director: Susan C. Thies
Editor: Mary L. Bush
Book Design: Tobi Cunningham
Cover Design: Mike Aspengren

With thanks to Diana Star Helmer and Sue Thies

IMAGE CREDITS
©CORBIS: p. 5; ©Reuters New Media Inc./CORBIS: pp.26–27, 37;
Library of Congress: pp. 9, 15, 19, 21, 22–23, 29, 32, 33; National
Archives: pp. 8, 13, 39; North Wind: p. 40

Corel: cover, pp. 4, 16–17, 18, 25, 34; Library of Congress: p. 35;
ArtToday (arttoday.com): pp. 1, 2–3, 6–7, 10–11, 12, 20, 26, 28, 30–31,
36, 38, 41, 42–43, 46, 48

For information, contact
Perfection Learning® Corporation
1000 North Second Avenue, P.O. Box 500,
Logan, Iowa 51546-0500.
Phone: 1-800-831-4190
Fax: 1-800-543-2745
perfection learning.com

1   2   3   4   5   BA   06   05   04   03   02

ISBN 0-7891-5839-6

TABLE OF CONTENTS

Chapter One

IN THE
BEGINNING

A Federal City

Did George Washington, America's first president, invent Washington, D.C.? Washington *did* have the big idea for a city that would be the center of American government. But it was Tobias Lear who was in charge of the actual details and plans.

Lear was Washington's secretary. His job was to write a booklet describing plans for the new **federal** city. Lear needed to sell the idea to the senators who would work there and the businessmen whose ships could trade there.

Congress had been meeting in many different cities. In 1783, Congress began discussing the idea of a "federal city."

George
Washington

Designing a Capital City

Washington hired Pierre Charles L'Enfant to design a capital city. L'Enfant was an officer for Washington during the Revolutionary War. The French architect had written to Washington in 1789. He explained that he was ready to create a

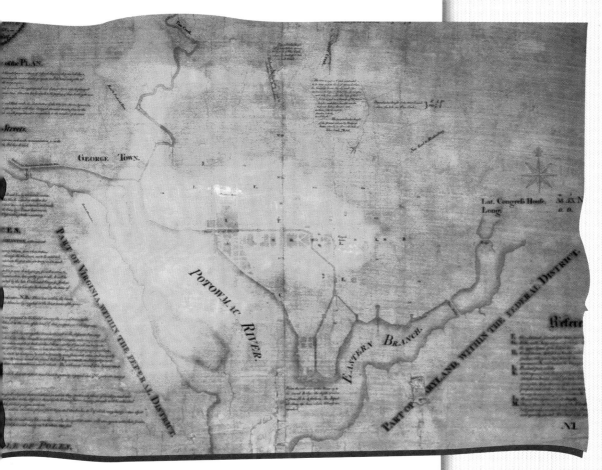

capital "magnificent enough to grace a great nation." Some of L'Enfant's ideas included five grand fountains with a constant flow of water and a statue of George Washington on horseback.

L'Enfant was hired in 1791. His first plans were for two main buildings—Congress House and the President's House (often called the "Executive Mansion"). L'Enfant's first design for the President's House was five times bigger than what was finally built. Some governors and congressmen claimed L'Enfant wanted to build a castle! In truth, L'Enfant was inspired by the French palace of Versailles.

Pierre Charles L'Enfant's plan for a Washington capital city

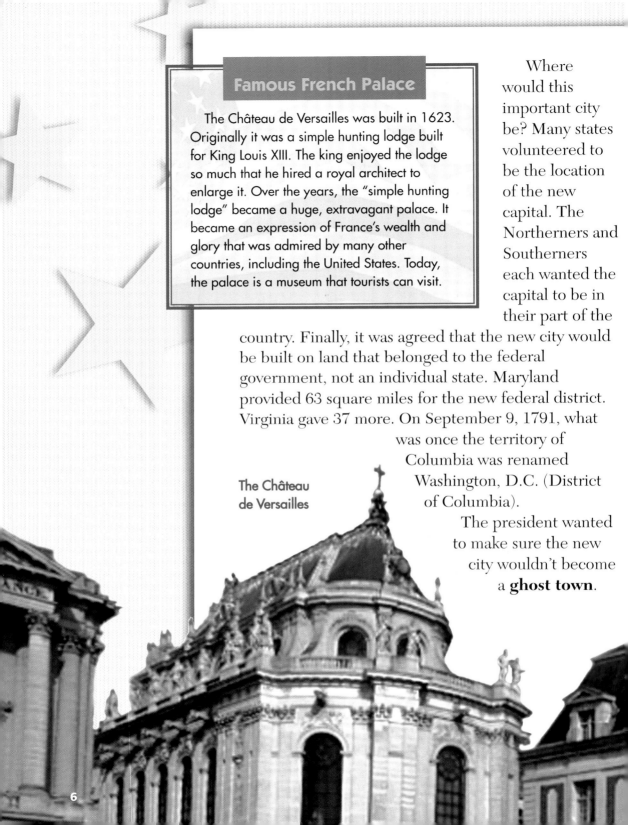

Where would this important city be? Many states volunteered to be the location of the new capital. The Northerners and Southerners each wanted the capital to be in their part of the country. Finally, it was agreed that the new city would be built on land that belonged to the federal government, not an individual state. Maryland provided 63 square miles for the new federal district. Virginia gave 37 more. On September 9, 1791, what was once the territory of Columbia was renamed Washington, D.C. (District of Columbia).

The president wanted to make sure the new city wouldn't become a **ghost town**.

The Château de Versailles

He ordered that all government workers must live in the city by 1800. This decision didn't affect many people. Besides elected officials, government workers included just 130 federal clerks.

The government hoped to sell **parcels** of land to help pay for construction. This plan led to more worries about L'Enfant's design for the city. L'Enfant wanted the main avenue, later known as Pennsylvania Avenue, to be 400 feet wide. Other streets would be 100 to 160 feet wide. Most American cities had streets just wide enough to let two carriages pass—perhaps 25 feet. Was L'Enfant's federal city plan wasting space that could be sold as more lots?

After only 11 months, city **commissioner** and future president Thomas Jefferson fired L'Enfant. Jefferson's fellow commissioner, Daniel Carroll, had bought land in the D.C. area and built a house on it. L'Enfant wanted that land to further his city design. When Carroll refused to tear down his house, L'Enfant tore it down himself! This was the end for L'Enfant.

After L'Enfant was fired, he was offered $2,500 and a parcel of land near the building that later became the White House. He refused. L'Enfant died poor in 1825. Not one of his building designs for the capital city was used.

When Secretary of the Treasury Oliver Wolcott Jr. moved to Washington in 1800, he was dismayed. While a few people lived like kings and the presidential buildings were extravagant, most of the population lived in poverty.

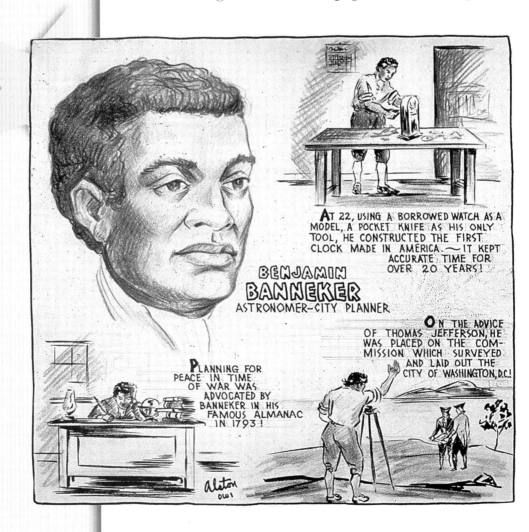

BENJAMIN BANNEKER
ASTRONOMER-CITY PLANNER

AT 22, USING A BORROWED WATCH AS A MODEL, A POCKET KNIFE AS HIS ONLY TOOL, HE CONSTRUCTED THE FIRST CLOCK MADE IN AMERICA. — IT KEPT ACCURATE TIME FOR OVER 20 YEARS!

ON THE ADVICE OF THOMAS JEFFERSON, HE WAS PLACED ON THE COMMISSION WHICH SURVEYED AND LAID OUT THE CITY OF WASHINGTON, D.C.!

PLANNING FOR PEACE IN TIME OF WAR WAS ADVOCATED BY BANNEKER IN HIS FAMOUS ALMANAC IN 1793!

Alston
OWI

Thanks, Benjamin Banneker!

Benjamin Banneker was a free black man who was skilled in many areas—astronomy, mathematics, engineering, inventing, and farming. At Thomas Jefferson's request, Banneker was appointed to the planning committee for Washington, D.C. When L'Enfant was fired, Banneker was able to reproduce from memory the plan for the streets, parks, and major buildings. Without him, Washington, D.C., would not exist as it does today.

He wrote of his shock:

There are few houses in any one place, and most of them small, miserable huts, which present an awful contrast to the public buildings. The people are poor, and as far as I can judge, they live like fishes, by eating each other.

This was not the "magnificent" city of any architect's dreams.

Not yet.

Washington

THE WHITE HOUSE

H ow did George Washington choose a new person to design the president's home? He held a contest to determine the best design. James Hoban entered the contest to design a house

for the president in 1792. The Irishman's design was inspired by Leinster Hall in Dublin and other Irish country houses. He won $500 and the chance to design the home of the president of the United States.

The first stone—the cornerstone—was laid for the "President's House" on October 13, 1792. The stone carried the Latin saying *"Vivat Republica,"* which means "Long live the **Republic**."

The President's House was white from its start.

South view of White House terrace in 1827

That's because the stone for the building was dug from a creek bed near the Potomac River and from nearby hillsides. This stone soaked up rain. Every winter, the rain-soaked stone would freeze and later crack. Covering the outside in whitewash was the best answer to the problem. That's why it was nicknamed the White House from the start. A vote from Congress made the name official in 1902.

Martha Washington

Abigail Adams

Dolley Madison

Finding workers to dig the stone and begin building proved difficult. Thomas Jefferson and the other two commissioners of the District of Columbia found that talented, big-city stonemasons were put off by the new city's lack of homes, churches, or even stores. Top builders didn't want to give up their good pay and comforts of home.

So the commissioners chose slave labor instead. Masters "rented" their slaves to the government. Slaves helped dig the clay and sand used to make bricks for construction.

The Presidents Move In

George Washington was not the first president to sleep in the White House. That honor belonged to second president John Adams and his wife, Abigail. Washington didn't live to see Adams move in, but his wife, Martha, did. She sent a servant with greetings and deer meat to the first White House occupants.

Mrs. Adams adjusted slowly to life in the official mansion. She described the upstairs East Room as a future "audience gathering room." But when her family first moved in, she used the East Room for drying laundry on indoor clotheslines!

Thomas Jefferson moved into the White House next. His wife had died years earlier. Jefferson began opening the White House to visitors twice yearly. The open houses were on New Year's Day and the Fourth of July. When hosting official dinners, Jefferson depended on Dolley Madison, the wife of Secretary of State James Madison, to act as hostess. When Madison **succeeded** Jefferson as president, Dolley knew her new home quite well.

Soon after Jefferson arrived in 1801, the new

president had two **water closets** installed upstairs at the White House. He wanted the outhouses torn down. When President Rutherford B. Hayes occupied the White House from 1877–1881, more modern bathrooms were added.

Even though most of the major construction on the White House was completed in 1829, the House keeps changing. New presidents make the home their own. When Bill Clinton was president, he ordered a jogging track built outside the White House.

The 132 rooms of the White House include some famous designs. Hoban studied President Washington's interests. He learned that Washington loved to greet guests standing in an oval formation. The idea for the rounded Oval Office was born, even though Washington never lived to see the results.

The Oval Office during the Jimmy Carter administration (1977–1981). Carter was the thirty-ninth president of the United States.

More than 1.5 million tourists now visit the White House yearly. Former President Franklin Roosevelt said, "I never forget that I live in a house owned by all the American people."

Today's capitol building began as nothing more than a spot on high ground. City architect L'Enfant noticed a hill that climbed 88 feet above the Potomac River. He called the area "a **pedestal** waiting for a monument."

Sixteen designs were offered by architects as plans for the Congress House, which was later renamed the Capitol. One designer whose work wasn't chosen called himself "Mr. AZ." Who was this architect? None other than Thomas Jefferson.

One of Jefferson's fellow commissioners, Doctor William Thornton, was chosen to design the capitol building. Thornton was from the West Indies. He was a physician and amateur architect. George Washington praised Thornton's building design for its "grandeur, simplicity, and convenience."

Construction Begins

President Washington laid the first stone of the Capitol in a ceremony on September 18, 1793. Oddly, the cornerstone has never been found. However, during a 1950s construction project, workers did find a fascinating bone at the site. The bone was the knee joint of a

Chapter Three

The Capitol

500-pound ox that had been roasted and eaten at the 1793 celebration.

Three years after construction began, funds ran out. The state of Maryland contributed more money. This money came from a lottery. People bought tickets in hopes of winning a cash prize. That's how the Capitol kept growing.

View of the U.S. Capitol and Pennsylvania Avenue before 1814

On November 21, 1800, thirty-two senators and one hundred and six representatives held their first meetings at the Capitol building. Only half of the building was completed at the time.

The Senate met in the finished north side. Members of the House of Representatives weren't so lucky. Their south side only had half-finished walls. So President Jefferson planned a temporary meeting place for the representatives. A one-story brick building was created *within the half-finished walls*! Congressmen nicknamed the small structure "the oven."

The north and south wings of the Capitol were connected by a central wooden porch area with two wells. After all, congressmen from the Senate or House all needed drinking water!

In 1814, a British invasion destroyed many of Washington's buildings, including the Capitol. Some Americans thought the government should be moved to another city. To keep this from happening, private citizens in Washington quickly built the "The Brick Capitol." This building, where the Supreme Court building now stands, was used until the Capitol was rebuilt and fully reopened in 1819.

The Rotunda

The Capitol's first dome, made of copper-covered wood, took its place between the Senate and the House in 1827. Beneath the dome was the Capitol Rotunda, a circular middle ground between the Houses. In the earliest days of the Rotunda, neither

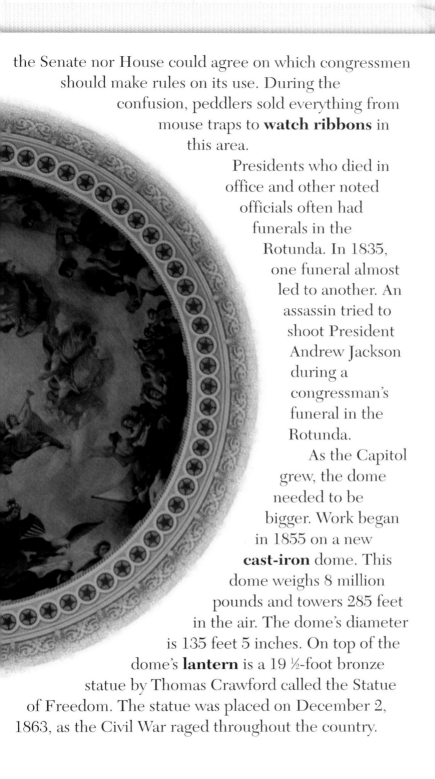

the Senate nor House could agree on which congressmen should make rules on its use. During the confusion, peddlers sold everything from mouse traps to **watch ribbons** in this area.

Presidents who died in office and other noted officials often had funerals in the Rotunda. In 1835, one funeral almost led to another. An assassin tried to shoot President Andrew Jackson during a congressman's funeral in the Rotunda.

As the Capitol grew, the dome needed to be bigger. Work began in 1855 on a new **cast-iron** dome. This dome weighs 8 million pounds and towers 285 feet in the air. The dome's diameter is 135 feet 5 inches. On top of the dome's **lantern** is a 19 ½-foot bronze statue by Thomas Crawford called the Statue of Freedom. The statue was placed on December 2, 1863, as the Civil War raged throughout the country.

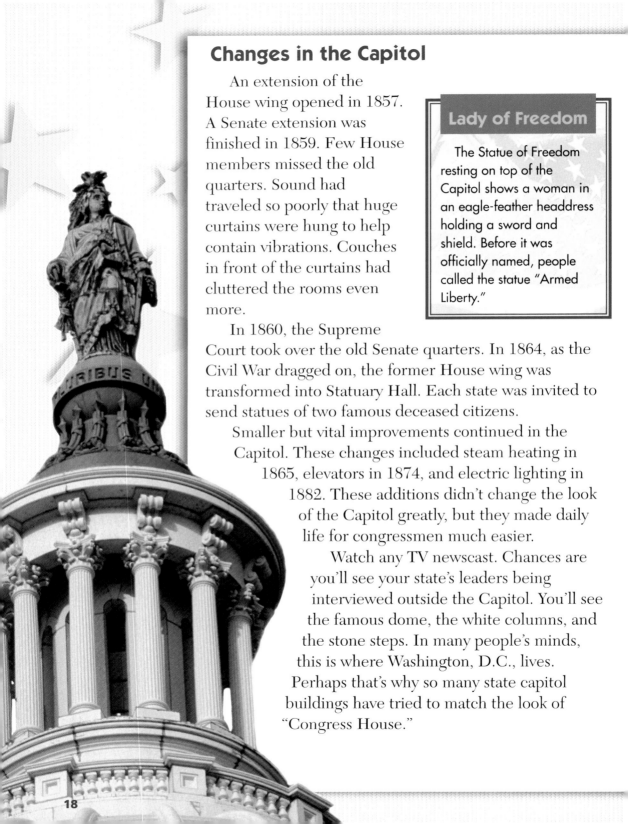

Changes in the Capitol

An extension of the House wing opened in 1857. A Senate extension was finished in 1859. Few House members missed the old quarters. Sound had traveled so poorly that huge curtains were hung to help contain vibrations. Couches in front of the curtains had cluttered the rooms even more.

In 1860, the Supreme Court took over the old Senate quarters. In 1864, as the Civil War dragged on, the former House wing was transformed into Statuary Hall. Each state was invited to send statues of two famous deceased citizens.

Smaller but vital improvements continued in the Capitol. These changes included steam heating in 1865, elevators in 1874, and electric lighting in 1882. These additions didn't change the look of the Capitol greatly, but they made daily life for congressmen much easier.

Watch any TV newscast. Chances are you'll see your state's leaders being interviewed outside the Capitol. You'll see the famous dome, the white columns, and the stone steps. In many people's minds, this is where Washington, D.C., lives. Perhaps that's why so many state capitol buildings have tried to match the look of "Congress House."

Lady of Freedom

The Statue of Freedom resting on top of the Capitol shows a woman in an eagle-feather headdress holding a sword and shield. Before it was officially named, people called the statue "Armed Liberty."

Chapter Four

A City Attacked!

I n 1812, America declared war on Great Britain. The British navy had been stopping American ships and kidnapping their sailors. At first, the British said they were looking for **deserters** who'd fled for better-paying jobs on American ships. But then innocent Americans were being taken and forced into British naval service.

On Wednesday, August 24, 1814, the British invaded Washington, D.C. What did American citizens do upon news of the invasion? Many wanted to watch! Just like a football game, crowds formed to see the soldiers from the two countries battle.

Under the command of General Robert Ross, the British forces attacked Washington, D.C., on August 24, 1814.

Even without modern technology, news of the British invasion traveled fast. British ships had landed in Maryland five days earlier. Some 5,000 invaders marched the 40 miles to Washington with hardly any American forces to oppose them.

The White House and Capitol Are Seized!

First Lady Dolley Madison was left alone in the White House while the president tried to inspect the city. Mrs. Madison depended on one servant and one sword to protect her. Before Dolley fled the White House in the afternoon, she insisted on bringing the portrait of George Washington. Fearing the invading British at any minute, Dolley instructed servants to break the frame and cut the canvas out of it. But as she fled to pack, servants safely loaded the entire life-sized portrait on a departing wagon. Dolley made sure her own painted portrait was saved too.

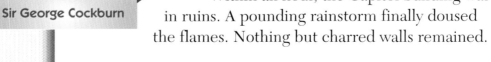

Sir George Cockburn led the British invaders. Entering the Capitol, Cockburn stood on the chair of the Speaker of the House of Representatives. "Shall this harbor of **Yankee** democracy be burned?" Cockburn asked his cheering men.

Cockburn bragged that he'd call on Mrs. Madison in her own White House **drawing room**. By midnight, the British made good on that promise and burned the "President's Palace." All the furniture, books, and other belongings of James and Dolley Madison were in flames.

Within an hour, the Capitol building was in ruins. A pounding rainstorm finally doused the flames. Nothing but charred walls remained.

Sir George Cockburn

Other Buildings Throughout the City

The country's largest collection of books, the Library of

Congress, was gone too. It burned in the Senate Building. British troops used the books as kindling for their bonfires.

The next morning, Doctor William Thornton, designer of the original Capitol building, found mercy from the British. Thornton begged Britain's Colonel Jones to spare the Patent Office, which Thornton himself had founded. He convinced the British soldiers that the building contained only private property and pleaded with the troops not to "burn what would be useful to all mankind . . ." The Patent Office, which also held the General Post Office, was the largest undamaged building remaining after the attack. Congress moved there until the temporary "Brick Capitol" was ready.

Britain's goal was to destroy all government property. So why did invading troops burn the city newspaper office? The British believed that all newspapers were run by the government. And Cockburn knew the newspaper had printed **editorials** against him. He told his men to destroy all the letter C blocks used on the printing presses so he'd never be criticized in print again!

A Patent, Please

A patent is an official document giving inventors exclusive rights to their inventions. This means that others can't make the same invention and claim that they invented it. A patent office is a government building where claims for patents are examined and granted.

The United States Patent Office in 1846

The End of the War

British soldiers claimed that only two private homes were destroyed. Supposedly, one house was torched after Americans fired upon British General Ross, shooting his horse. When the Americans wouldn't surrender, the house where they were hiding was burned. The second home burned "by accident" because it was too close to the blazing Capitol.

The British retreated to their ships early the next day. They feared that the stormy weather and a possible American **counterattack** could end their invasion success.

Reports claimed that Washington, D.C., had suffered $30 million in damages. On Christmas Eve, 1814, both countries signed a peace treaty. The war was over. Neither

White House in 1814

side won land or anything else. Both countries agreed to return to prewar conditions.

But the scars of war didn't disappear overnight. For the next 2 ½ years, President Madison and his wife lived in rented homes around Washington. Six months after President James Monroe's 1817 inauguration, a first family was finally allowed to move into the rebuilt White House.

Famous Firsts

The term *first family* is used to describe the wife and children of the current president. *First lady* refers to the president's wife.

Chapter Five

More Washington, D.C., Landmarks

As the country grew, so did Washington, D.C. In 1836, work on the Treasury Building began. Robert Mills, who later designed the Washington Monument, created this design. His vision was inspired by Greek architecture.

Pierre Charles L'Enfant had thought that the corner of F and Seventh Streets was the perfect place for a national church and **mausoleum**. Instead, construction started in 1837 to build the Patent Office there. The site later turned into the Civil Service Commission.

Railway service reached the city in 1835. Within three years, passengers could travel between the nation's capital and New York. In 1846, telegraph service was added. With communication and transportation, the District of Columbia grew. Between 1800 and 1840, the population climbed from 14,000 to 44,000.

Library of Congress

After the British invasion of 1814, Thomas

Civil Service Commission

Civil Service refers to nonmilitary people who work in government jobs. Civil Service employees are given jobs based on their qualifications and skills rather than being elected. To make sure that jobs were given to people in a fair manner, the Civil Service Act was passed in 1883. The government then established the Civil Service Commission to enforce the law.

Jefferson sold his personal collection of 6,700 books to Congress for $23,700. But then another disaster struck America's library. An 1851 fire reduced the Library of Congress collection from 55,000 to 20,000. More than 4,000 of Jefferson's books were lost in the blaze. In 1897, a building was constructed to house just the Library of Congress. Before, these books were stored in the Capitol.

The Smithsonian

One of the most unique buildings from 1800s Washington is "The Castle." That's the nickname for the first building of the Smithsonian Institution. A British scientist named James Smithson donated more than a half million dollars in gold coins to found "an establishment for the increase and **diffusion** of knowledge." Congress debated from 1838 to 1846 if it was proper to accept such a donation from a **foreigner**. At last, in 1855, the red sandstone headquarters was built.

A Trip to the Smithsonian

If you took a trip to Washington, D.C., today, you could spend weeks just visiting the Smithsonian's 14 museums and galleries as well as the National Zoo. Some of these museums include the National Air and Space Museum, the National Museum of American History, and the National Museum of Natural History. The National Gallery of Art, the Hirshhorn Museum and Sculpture Garden, and the Freer Gallery of Art are a few of the Smithsonian art galleries. Two additional Smithsonian museums are located in New York City.

The Smithsonian Institution building is home to over 140 million items of historical or artistic importance.

Blair House

Another red structure in the city has a famous past. Blair House is located at 1651 Pennsylvania Avenue—on the same block as the White House. Blair House was built by a city doctor between 1824 and 1827. In 1836, Francis Blair, editor of the *Globe* newspaper, bought the red brick home. President Harry Truman lived there from 1948 through 1952 when the White House was being remodeled. A policeman died at Blair House in 1950 stopping an assassination attempt against Truman. Today, it's the presidential guest quarters. Visiting foreign leaders stay there.

President Harry Truman was the thirty-third president of the United States.

Modern D.C.

When did Washington start looking like modern cities of today? The first apartment house was built in 1879. By that time, more than 100 government offices had "electric speaking telephones." The first electric lights in city buildings were used in 1881. Residents rode the first electric streetcar in 1888. Today, Washington, D.C., is a booming city with condos, cell phones, brightly lit office

buildings, cars, and a glittering entertainment world.

In spite of its modern progress, Washington, D.C., has remained a city of history. In 1937, when the government published a book entitled *Washington: City and Capital*, the writers tracked down more than 500 historical statues, monuments, and memorials throughout the city. While it takes people to make history, people often want buildings to remember that history—and to make history in!

The Blair House in January of 2001

The Washington Monument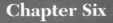

In Honor of George

Tourist Lewis Beebe visited Washington in the summer of 1800. He kept a diary, highlighting his findings. In this crowded, growing place, Beebe noted an undisturbed stretch of land. From the Potomac River to the White House, Pierre Charles L'Enfant had left a clearing of high ground. Beebe predicted that a mausoleum would be built there for use when George Washington died.

Beebe's prediction was partly right. The land *did* become the site of the Washington Monument—but the monument was not a mausoleum.

Congress first wanted to honor the Revolutionary War hero in 1783. At that time, Congress approved the idea of a statue of Washington in a chariot driving four horses! But the humble George Washington objected to federal money being spent to honor him.

Washington died in 1799. In 1835, a contest was held to design a national monument in his honor. Robert Mills won. Much of his design was changed as the monument progressed.

This statue of George Washington stands in the U.S. Capitol Rotunda.

Mills' idea of a huge tower, or obelisk, endured.

Estimates said that more than $1 million would be needed. Volunteers asked for one-dollar "subscriptions" from citizens across the country. Unfortunately, only $30,000 was raised this way.

Construction Begins

In 1848, Congress granted land for the Washington Monument. The cornerstone was laid July 4, 1848, using a **trowel** that George Washington had held in the cornerstone dedication at the Capitol. Soon after, the monument's designers ended up moving the site because the ground in the original spot was too soft to support the tall building.

As construction began, the Monument Society kept seeking cash donations. Then they came up with a new idea. Groups could donate stones. The stones came from groups around the world. Messages were carved on about 190 of these stones to be used in the monument's construction. The messages can still be read inside the monument today.

Benjamin B. French laid the cornerstone of the Washington Monument. French was a mason (skilled stone and brick layer) who held several important goverment positions in Washington.

Pope Pius IX of Italy donated a block of marble from a temple in Rome for the monument. But on the night of March 5, 1854, masked men from the American Party, nicknamed the Know-Nothings, stole the block. The American Party was against foreign or religious involvement in United States government issues. The protest finished with the thieves smashing the stone and tossing the pieces into the nearby Potomac River.

The same hate group broke into the Monument Society offices on February 21, 1855. They elected new officers and vowed to complete the monument as "an American institution, supported by all Americans." Congress refused to provide a promised $200,000 to complete construction. Public donations dried up as well. Two years later, the original members of the official society regained control.

The Monument Is Completed

A lack of funds and the Civil War caused the half-built monument to sit neglected for 15 years. This explains why the color of stone changes slightly on the tallest third of the monument. Finally in 1876, the one hundredth anniversary of the signing of the Declaration of Independence sparked new patriotism. Congress supplied the needed $200,000, and the monument was completed.

The **capstone** was placed on December 6, 1884. The

monument towered 555 feet 5 ⅛ inches. The aluminum tip of the capstone was displayed beforehand in New York and Washington. Some amazed sightseers asked to step over the 8.9-inch tip. Why? So they could claim that they had stepped over the "top" of the Washington Monument!

By the time building was complete, the cost topped $1.5 million. The monument opened to the public on October 9, 1888. Government engineers proudly noted that the monument made of 36,491 blocks of marble could withstand a 145-mile-per-hour tornado wind.

In 1901, steam-powered elevators could transport tourists to the top of the monument in five minutes. Current electric elevators get visitors to the top in 60 seconds.

In the beginning, only men were allowed on the elevators. Because elevators were potentially dangerous, women had to walk the stairs if they wanted to enjoy the view from the monument's top. Currently, the National Park Service doesn't allow any tourist to walk up the stairs. The Park Service was worried about the safety of tourists on the long stairways. Many people suffered heart attacks from the lengthy climb.

Whether they ride to the top or just enjoy the view from the ground, tourists still come from all over to visit this tribute to the nation's first president.

Chapter Seven

Days to Remember in D.C.

Every day seems like a big day in Washington, D.C. Whenever Congress is meeting, laws are discussed changed, or made. From his Oval Office, the president makes important decisions that affect the nation.

But sometimes, the "everyday" people of the capital city change history. Some of these changes have brought hope and justice. Others brought shock and sadness.

The Right To Vote

One woman assembled 8,000 marchers for a parade in the capital city on March 3, 1913. A crowd of half a million people attended the event. How could one parade draw so many observers? Organizer Alice Paul said the city had never hosted an all-women parade before. But it wasn't ust a simple celebration. Miss Paul wanted bands, floats, and other parade entries to show different aspects of women's lives. She was leading the campaign to change the laws so women would have the right to vote.

The huge crowd turned into a near riot. Marchers were shoved and injured as 175 ambulances were called. The march wasn't orderly, but it got the city's attention. Congress discussed women's suffrage for the first time in 35 years. In 1920, the Nineteenth Amendment to the Constitution gave women the right to vote.

The Great Depression

Beginning in 1929, Americans faced The Great Depression. The stock market crashed, jobs were hard to find, and many people were homeless and penniless. These hard times lasted for many years.

In the summer of 1932, more than 25,000 soldiers from World War I gathered in Washington, bringing their wives and children. They came to ask Congress to pay them the bonus promised to veterans in 1924. Under the plan, benefits would not be paid until 1945. But the veterans needed the money and the hope immediately.

The protesters called themselves the Bonus Expeditionary Force (BEF). They pitched tents and built shacks with their families along Pennsylvania Avenue near the White House. They were poor, hungry, and jobless. And they weren't leaving.

Bonus Expeditionary Force demonstration on the steps of the Capitol on July 2, 1932

President Herbert Hoover never talked with the protesters. Instead, he called his troops. The Third Cavalry arrived on horseback, ready to fight protesters. The U.S. Army followed, using tanks and tear gas. The commanding officers were General Douglas MacArthur and Major George Patton, who later became heroes of World War II.

In one night, the protester camp was crushed and burned. Three people died. Not a single veteran was paid.

A Great Memorial for a Great Man

The Lincoln Memorial honors the nation's sixteenth president, Abraham Lincoln. This building was modeled after Greek temples. Thirty-six columns representing the thirty-six states in the Union at the time support the monument's roof. Inside sits a marble statue of Lincoln. Paintings and writings that symbolize Lincoln's great achievements cover the walls.

I Have a Dream

The most famous speech ever made by an unelected leader in the capital city came in 1963. On August 28, 1963, about 250,000 people gathered in front of the Lincoln Memorial in Washington, D.C. They wanted laws passed to protect the civil rights of all people of all races. Reverend Martin Luther King Jr.'s "I Have a Dream" speech about the future highlighted the day.

Martin Luther King Jr. won the 1964 Nobel Peace Prize for his nonviolent leadership in the black fight for equality.

The Death of a President

That same year, America lost a president. On November 21, 1963, President John F. Kennedy flew to Texas to give several speeches. The next day, as his car slowly drove past cheering crowds in Dallas, gunshots followed. Kennedy was hit. He died a short time later. His casket was placed in the East Room of the White House, where assassinated President Abraham Lincoln's body had lain nearly 100 years before.

A Place of Honor and Remembrance

Arlington National Cemetery is a military cemetery where more than 260,000 people are buried. Beginning with the American Revolution, veterans from all of the nation's wars are laid to rest in this cemetery. On average, 20 funerals a day take place at Arlington. The cemetery is also open to visitors.

On November 23, hundreds of thousands of people stood in the rainy mist to watch a horse-drawn carriage take the assassinated leader's body from the White House to the National Cathedral for the funeral. Kennedy was then buried in Arlington National Cemetery.

Marble sculpture of John F. Kennedy

Tomb of the Unknowns

Also known as the Tomb of the Unknown Soldier, this tomb holds the remains of three unidentified soldiers—one each from World War I, World War II, and the Vietnam War. The "unidentified" soldier from the Vietnam War was actually identified later (1998) through DNA testing. Although the body was **exhumed**, it was decided that the crypt, or chamber, of the Vietnam soldier will remain intact and vacant.

Hijacked!

After Great Britain's 1814 attack, the capital city wasn't struck again until Tuesday, September 11, 2001. A passenger airplane from Washington's Dulles Airport was headed to Los Angeles. But the plane was hijacked by terrorists and crashed into the western side of the Pentagon at 10:43 a.m. A violent fire burned through the building. The plane was carrying 58 passengers and 6 crew. There were no survivors.

Nearly 25,000 people work in the five-sided military headquarters. More than a hundred died in the explosion.

Another hijacked passenger plane crashed in Pennsylvania. The **FBI** believes that terrorists may have hoped to crash that plane into the White House or Capitol.

Every day, people come to Washington, D.C., to be seen and heard. No one knows what messages they might bring or what the results might be. History happens one day—and one person—at a time.

The Pentagon after terrorist attack on September 11, 2001

Chapter Eight

Party for the President

Imagine your city or town having a huge party once every four years. People around the world anticipate the celebration. They wait for news of what happened at the party.

That's how important **inaugurations** in Washington, D.C., are. Every four years, a president begins a new term in office. That four-year term begins with a ceremony, parade, and celebration.

The Tradition Begins

The tradition began on March 4, 1801. Thomas Jefferson had been elected president. Philadelphia planned its own parade. City leaders still hoped that Philadelphia could regain its position as the nation's capital. After all, previous inaugurations had been held there.

The first signs of celebration in Washington came when the Washington Artillery Company began firing its muskets to mark the occasion. They were

Thomas Jefferson

joined by the Alexandria Company. Soldiers paraded outside the Conrad and McMunn's tavern, where President Jefferson rented a room. (Former President John Adams didn't move out of the White House until the morning of the swearing in, so Jefferson needed other sleeping quarters.)

Jefferson and his friends appeared outside the tavern some two hours after the soldiers passed. They walked to the Capitol. This wasn't the fancy type of parade Philadelphia had planned. It wasn't long either. The tavern advertised itself as "200 paces from the Capitol."

Presidential Firsts

The next time a president would get such inaugural exercise was in 1977. President Jimmy Carter was the first to walk with his family back to the White House from the Capitol after the swearing in ceremony.

James Madison's inauguration on March 4, 1809, began with a blast. Cannons were fired that morning at the Naval Yard. The

President Jimmy Carter and First Lady Rosalynn Carter walk down Pennsylvania Avenue.

streets of Washington filled with more than 10,000 onlookers. After Madison's inaugural speech, nine volunteer **militia** units waited outside to be inspected by their new leader.

Another kind of "blast" was created by First Lady Dolley Madison. Mrs. Madison was the first to plan an "inaugural ball," a dance that has become a tradition. When President Clinton was inaugurated in 1993, supporters held 13 different inaugural balls around the city. The Clintons danced at every one!

The 1800s saw many changes in the inaugural ceremony. In 1817, James Monroe was the first president to swear the oath of office outside (where crowds could watch). In 1825, John Quincy Adams was the first president to wear long pants to the ceremony instead of knee-length knickers. Lincoln's inaugural parade was the first to allow African Americans to participate. James Garfield was the first president to sit in a stand outside the White House to witness the inaugural parade in 1881. In 1917, President Woodrow Wilson's parade was the first to include women.

Abraham Lincoln

Abraham Lincoln's 1865 inauguration could have ended in tragedy. Lincoln walked through the Capitol that day. He was escorted by

Inauguration of Abraham Lincoln on steps of U.S. Capitol

many government officials. The Commissioner of Public Buildings saw a man jump out of the crowd. The man insisted on walking behind the president as the group headed toward the swearing-in ceremony on the Capitol's east side. The commissioner ordered policemen to escort the man away from the president.

Only after President Lincoln was shot and killed at a theater later that year did Commissioner Benjamin French remember that face. He had seen assassin John Wilkes Booth on inauguration day. Photos of Lincoln's inaugural speech show Booth hovering in the crowd.

John Wilkes Booth

January 20

Since 1933, Washington's inauguration day has occurred on January 20. The Twentieth Amendment of the Constitution was changed to note that a new president must start his term on that day. Franklin D. Roosevelt was the first inaugurated on January 20. He was the first and *only* president inaugurated four times!

The second inauguration of Franklin D. Roosevelt

That January date isn't always the warmest for celebrating. In 1961, snow threatened President John F. Kennedy's inaugural parade. Pennsylvania Avenue was cleared by the army, who used flame throwers to melt the snow! In 1985, Ronald Reagan was the first to take the oath in the Capitol Rotunda. The temperature outside was -2° F.

But no matter the weather or the president, Washington, D.C., knows one thing. It only has to wait four more years for the next inauguration celebration. Then once again, the great city can throw a party to honor the nation's past and future.

Internet Connections to Washington, D.C.

http://www.cityspin.com/washington_dc/index.htm
Visit Washington, D.C., online through these links to the city's sights and "City Kids," things for younger people to enjoy.

http://www.whitehousekids.gov
This official president's Web site for students takes you on a tour of the White House; provides information on the nation's capital, presidents, and American heroes; and tests your knowledge of the United States with a fun history quiz.

http://memory.loc.gov/ammem/pihtml/pihome.html
The Library of Congress created this "I Do Solemnly Swear . . ." site, which is a history of presidential inaugurations. Many photos, sound clips, and video highlights make past ceremonies come alive again.

To mail a letter to the president or a member of the president's family, send your letter to the following address:

White House
1600 Pennsylvania Avenue Northwest
Washington, D.C. 20500-0003

capstone	stone placed at the top of a building
cast-iron	a mixture of iron, carbon, and silicon that results in a hard, unbendable metal
commissioner	representative of the government
counterattack	attack in response or retaliation to a previous attack
deserter	person who leaves military service without official approval
diffusion	scattering or spreading
drawing room	formal reception (greeting) room
editorial	newspaper or magazine article that presents the opinions of the author
exhumed	taken out of a grave or tomb
FBI	Federal Bureau of Investigation; chief investigating branch of the United States government

federal	relating to a central government
foreigner	person who comes from a country other than one's own
ghost town	town with no one or almost no one living in it
inauguration	a ceremonial beginning for someone taking an elected office
lantern	small tower
mausoleum	building that houses the bodies of dead people
militia	group of citizens organized for military service
parcel	plot, or area, of land
pedestal	base or foundation, often on a high level
republic	government having elected officials
riot	public fighting, usually involving large groups of people

succeeded	followed in office
suffrage	right to vote
trowel	hand tool used to apply, spread, shape, or smooth materials
veteran	person who has served in a war
watch ribbon	decorative attachment for a pocket watch
water closet	room or area used for toilet facilities
Yankee	person from or living in the United States

Index